For Sowmya, Mariya, Seema and Abhinaya
who live in the heavens and in my heart

Luckily
Woman
by birth
And then you
accept me
in fact
freedom I
do not recite
gyno-grammar
have crafted
self
I am at any

Contents

Contents

Author's Note

This book is a bundle of so many of my emotions – joy, pain, anger, fury, distress and hope. Through this book, I tell some parts of my story and that of the others like me. You will hear their voices through me.

Poetry and art give a richness to my life. They give beauty, strength and hope. They heal. I couldn't have survived my tormented teenage years without them.

This book is a collection of poems, articles, illustrations, monologues and some real conversations that have actually happened in my life. In here, you will read my original English poems and poems which were first written by me in Thamizh and later translated to English.

In 2014, my collection of Thamizh poems were published as *'Kuri Aruthean'* by Vikatan publishers.

Eight poems from that collection were translated by my great friend and mentor **N.Elango**. His translations are *Nirvaanam, A mutilated vagina called Eezham, Arise my precious, Clap aloud, Kali Maha Kali, Amma, Phallus I cut* and *Fate I wrote*. Two poems *'If you don't mind'* and *'Half a woman' were translated by me*. This book also includes my original handwritten scripts of the Tamil poems.

I thank my dear friend, scholar artivist **Laura Sherwood** for her critical feedback and appreciation of my art and poetry during the development of this book. I thank my mother **Rajamani** for her immense care of me and her advice while writing this book and forever. I also thank my dear friend **N. Senthil Kumar** for being a guide in the making this book.

– **Kalki Subramaniam**

Foreword

It was a beautiful morning in the year 2013. I wasn't conscious of what happened that day epochs ago. How would I know what he would have felt, subsequent to the violently passionate sex, he, the bachelor-warrior epochs ago knowing that he was going to die the next morning … not mortally wounded by enemy's arrow or spear, but sacrificed to the god of war, in a ritual known as *'Kalapali'* ('field-sacrifice')

What would I know about the pain of that beautiful young woman who would have bathed in the high end of pleasure by the fierce love of her young husband, as she knows that her husband would be and she would be widowed in the morning.? The betrayal she would have suffered in a cosmic game played by men where she was thrown into oblivion, passionless, lifeless and even nameless, forgotten by the great epics and Vedas and Puranas which deified only her one-night-stand husband Aravan as *Koothandavar*.

That morning when I opened my Facebook, I was frozen. There in a news feed was this stunningly beautiful woman, in red saree, with her olive face and the vermillion on her forehead hastily rubbed-off, leaving its trace still on that broad forehead, and she was looking straight into my eyes. I couldn't take my eyes off her face. As my eyes slowly lowered, unable to stand the surge of a flood of strange feeling gushing to drown me in it, I found her Tamil poem typed beneath her image titled *'Vidhiyai Ezhudhinaen'*. It was a poem on her daring decision not to participate in the ritual performed and participated by all transgender women in India. She had decided not to perform the mock-wedding and voluntarily undergo widowhood by severing the nuptial knot in the morning. As I finished reading that poem, a lump had formed in my throat

11

and even if I swallowed saliva, I could feel the pain in my throat. Though it was a working day, and I engaged my classes in The American College, I was in a perpetual daze. I couldn't concentrate on anything. The relief came to me only after I translated her poem in to English titled as *'Fate, I Wrote'* and posted it on my Facebook wall. A couple of days later there was a call and a voice resonated "Hello sir, I am Kalki speaking". Once again, I grew nervous. I am not able to recollect now any other word spoken by her except that she was satisfied with my translation.

Subsequently I translated another poem of hers, *'Kuri Aruthaen'* as *'Phallus, I Cut'*. Then, after a few days R. P. Nair, my former professor and the editor of *Kavya Bharati*, a journal for poetry, from the internationally reputed study centre, SCILET (Study Centre for Indian Literature in English and Translation) called me and offered to publish *'Fate, I* Wrote'.

Then came many of her poems, not from the wailing fields of Koothandavar Festivals. But as she herself swore in *'Fate, I Wrote'* and *'Phallus, I Cut'*, they were clarion calls, not only to the LGBT community, but for those whosoever seek to break themselves free from the shackles and fetters snapped around them by the hegemonic conspiracy.

Many a time I have struggled to translate her vernacular images, such as the one in *'Phallus, I Cut'*: "*Maathavam aedhum seyavillai, Mangayarai pirappadhaRku*" which is an allusion to the line "*Mangayarai pirappadhaRkae nalla maathavam seydhida vaendumamma*" from the celebrated Tamil poet Kavimani Desika Vinayagam Pillai. Whereas Kavimani claims one should do great penance to be born blessed as a woman, I had to be content with myself in this translation: "No transcendental meditation did I perform/ to transform myself in to a woman…". But I will be content only with my translation, not for the immeasurable love I have for the poet and the unbounded joy I feel in being a part of her great mission.

In all these years, I have met Kalki only once, that too in a conference, and I have talked to her over the phone only a couple of times. But her poems and in the process of translating them, I have been actually holding her very close to me and have been reading her metaphorically inch by inch from the strand of her hair to the toe-nail. When I saw her painting 'Piece by Piece' that is akin to Cubism I could just get as close to reading the soul of it.

Today many academic institutions have started prescribing her poems. I am sure many would feel as I do now. But I would always tell myself that it was I who held her so close to me first.

– N.Elango

Founder-Director of Fourth Wall Theatre,
(Former)Head, Postgraduate Department of English,
The American College, Madurai.
(Hon.) Head, Postgraduate Department of English,
Mannar Thirumalai Naicker College,
Madurai.

Special Notes

Kalki is a brilliant artist, activist, and all-around Super-Shero Artivist! This book challenges the cis-privilege narrative. Kalki poetically weaves the complexities and struggles transgender people experience and pours her heart and soul into every page of this book, permitting the reader to grasp the anguish, anger, and injustices that transgender people endure in their daily lives.

The personal narratives in this book demonstrate the lived experiences from an insider's perspective. Too often, researchers or outsiders tell the story of the "other" from their own limited point of view, resulting in the propagation of stereotypes and "othering" of those who don't fit the hegemonic gender binary narrative. This book is essential for all academic institutions and programs working to dismantle dominant narratives or facilitate dialogue around gender beyond the binary.

I have had the privilege of working with Kalki on multiple creative projects over the last four years. She is one of my dearest friends and my favorite person on the planet! Her endless passion, commitment, and creativity continually inspire me to want to do and be more.

Our first face-to-face introduction started with a Kalki greeting me with a flower and with a sweet cup of chai. In 2018 I travelled from the United States to India, where I spent two weeks with Kalki in her hometown of Pollachi.

In 2017 I reached out to Kalki, expressing my interest in her artistic activism with the transgender community. Kalki graciously agreed to collaborate with me for research and invited me to India, where she welcomed me into her home. Since this time we have become dear friends. From the onset of the global pandemic, we have connected via video chat almost daily, creating art, dancing, and sharing everything from recipes to relationships.

It's been an enlightening experience to witness Kalki's ability to transition from one medium to another. Like a beautiful piece of music, her artwork inspires deep reflection. Kalki's artistic visual storytelling seeks to reach the hearts and minds of those who would otherwise not be exposed to the messages imparted through Kalki's artwork.

There are no words that can express the love and gratitude I feel for Kalki. I have great adoration for the phenomenal Artivist that she is.

Sincerely,

– Laura Sherwood Ph.D.

Human and Organizational Development
Founder of the Non-profit Transformative Arts Project
Aspiring Artivist and Transgender Ally.

I speak
because we need
to be heard,

I write
because we need
to be understood,

I dare
because we need
to survive.

– Kalki –

If You Don't Mind

(and I hope he really didn't mind)

"Friend…?"

"Yes, *Thozhar**…"

"If you don't mistake me
shall I ask you a question?"

"Yes please, ask!
I won't take it badly"

"Are your breasts real?"

"Mm…" (awkward silence)

"Oh I see……
If you won't mind, can I ask
another question?"

"Mm……" ("*shoot your prerogative again*", I whisper to myself)

---

*   *Thozhar is a Thamizh word which means Comrade.*

"Do you have a vagina?
Does it look like a woman's?"

"Mm…
Thozhar…?"

"Yes friend!"

"If you won't take it as an offence,
shall I ask you something?"

"Don't hesitate to ask me *Thozhar*,
I won't take it in offensively"

"Do you have a prick?"

முன் குறிப்பு

தோழி ?

சொல்லுங்கள் தோழர்

தவறாக நினைத்தவில்லையெனில்
ஒன்று கேட்கட்டுமா?

கேளுங்கள் தோழர்
தவறாமல் நினைக்க மாட்டேன்

உங்தள் மார்பு உண்மையா?

ம்...

ஏ
தவறாக நினைக்கவில்லையெனில்
இன்னொரு கேள்வி

ம்...

உங்களுக்கு பெண்குறி உண்டா?
பெண்ணைப் போலவா?

ம்... தோழர் ?

சொல்லுங்கள் தோழி.....

தவறாக நினைக்கவில்லையெனில்
ஒன்று கேட்கட்டுமா?

தயங்காமல் கேளுங்கள் தோழி
தவறாக நினைக்கமாட்டேன்

உங்களுக்கு ஆண்குறி உண்டா?

She

Her turmeric face
was glowing
with the crimson red *Kungumam*[*]
centered on her forehead
like a blazing sun,
she wore a rustling
green saree that was flowing
as if she had wings.

She clapped,
she walked
from car to car,
she tapped the glass
and clapped
so they could hear her
and give her money.

They were all grim and caged,
and trapped in their pasts
and uncertain futures,

_____

[*]   *Kungumam is the red dot kept between the two eyes brows, also known as bindi or
      sintoor.*

she was the only one
free and present.

She clapped
and clapped for herself,
she walked free.

It is okay to be a

gay, lesbian or

It is okay to be

or white. What

is being

and inhuman

⚧ transgender,

bisexual person.

black, brown

is not okay

judgemental

about it.

Don't Tell That to Me

I am tired of you
telling me
how I don't look like
a transgender woman.

I am tired of you
telling me
I look just like
a real woman.

I am tired of you
telling me
I am so brave.

I am tired of you
telling me
everything is perfect
except my voice
which could be more feminine.

I am tired of you
asking me
when was the first time
I felt that I am a transgender.

I am tired of you
asking me
if I live with my family.

I am tired of your
Curiosity.

I am tired of your
Sympathy.

I am tired of
your stare.

I am tired of your
whispers.

I am tired of you
asking me
to bless you.

To you and to
the million others
I want to shout
I am made of
flesh and blood,
of fear and hope,
of joy and pain.

I am like you
I am human too.

A Little Girl and Me

"Hello Kalki aunty"

"Hi Chellamma"

"Shall we play in the garden?"

"Yes yes… I am ready baby.
Let me pick up the rings and rope"

"Aunty…?"

"Yes sweety?"

"You are a beautiful lady. Why is your voice like a boy's?

"Because Chellamma, I was born a boy, suffered much and I became
a girl."

"Is it aunty…?"

"Yes dear"

"Okay aunty. Come let us play"

Will an Indian Man Ever Bring a Trans Woman Home and Say 'Ma, I Love Her'?

"Look at the men who crave for us. If we are desirable for lust, why not love? Don't we deserve it?" said Priya, one of my friends, a trans woman. She always desired to have a husband, children, and a big band of in-laws. Shunned away by her own biological family because of her coming out as trans, she now lives alone struggling for a livelihood, struggling for a dignified place in society.

For most transgender women like me, marital life is often just a dream which never becomes a reality. In 2009, when a mainstream matrimonial website rejected my profile, I started a matrimony website for transgender women. When I first launched a Thirunangai Transgender Matrimonial website, with just six profiles of trans women, we were flooded with 2,000 marriage proposals. These proposals were pouring in from all around the world, but mostly from India. It was the world's first matrimonial website for trans women.

Hundreds of Indian men were ready to marry trans women. Many of the proposal emails were accompanied by their photographs, short bio, and their expectations in a relationship. We received proposals from diverse cultural backgrounds, men who were scientists, business owners, professors, IT professionals, doctors, engineers, and even astrologers, men from different religions and faiths, and communities. We were elated at the huge response we got within two weeks of the website launch. Two thousand proposals for six transgender spinsters!! (I was the one who got a higher number of proposals.)

We had announced some terms and conditions through our website. We had clearly stated that we will not give any kind of dowry. We also stated that the wedding has to be public and proposals for secret marriages would be outright dismissed.

Different transwomen have different needs in a relationship. Many of us have been ostracized by our own biological families for being trans. We need love, we could give love and receive it, we have a lust for life and longings like all cisgender girls. Above all, we deserve to be in homes, not on the streets begging and doing sex work, right? We deserve to have a husband and a family, don't we?

Unfortunately, most of the Indian men who proposed to us through our website wanted a secret marriage. "You see Kalki ma'am, I love and respect transgender women, I am ready to marry one too, but my family will be hurt if they come to know," said an IT guy. "I will face problems with my business if I have an open marriage," said a businessman.

From princes to paupers, all the Indian men who sent their proposals for marriage had no issues with marrying a trans woman, but they all came with their only tag – 'Secret Marriage'. We were filled with tons of excitement and our heads were filled with silk draped dreams to be the bahus. After several rounds of interviews with the men over telephone and email (we never met them in person), reality dawned on us slowly. 'Secret Marriage', 'Secret Relationship', 'Secret Love', 'Secret Wife', Secret Secret Secret! That is what they want. Aargh…

There were many other (un)interesting proposals too. A millionaire oily sheik from Dubai wrote to me: "I will take you as my third wife, I will give you everything you want." I felt so low. No amount of his oiling could lubricate and melt my heart. I didn't want to be his mistress, no way!

An English teacher wanted to marry one of the profiled girls, Sowmya. He wrote "I have a bedridden wife and I am impotent too. I just need someone to take care of my wife and me. I can give whatever Sowmya wants."

I was hesitant, but I needed to tell Sowmya this. I spoke to her about this proposal and she just glared at me, all red in the face. "Kalki, are you nuts? You @#$*& @#%$@!!" Words came like fireworks from her. I wanted to hide under the table. Never did I speak to her about this again.

Many transgender women desire a married life. They believe it brings respect, peace, love, and security for the rest of their lives and above all a meaning to life. However, we do not have legal protection for such marriages. The growing acceptance in society is a positive change, however, a secured marriage and adopting a child may remain a dream for a very long time.

After hundreds of failed interviews and eventually gulping big coffee cups of disappointment, the six of us had a final meeting. We decided we don't need secret yellow threads of marriage hanging on our chests. We were vulnerable to be manipulated and yellow threads could turn into an iron chain, we decided.

I told the girls "These guys who want secret marriages just don't get it. What difference does it make for us in such relationships? It will be unfulfilling, the guy could leave us anytime and we will be left out with nothing, no one, no protection, and no justice."

Monal, one of the girls, said "Let's roll back our hopes and wait for the day people change. We will open their eyes, and open their hearts. Until then we shall continue to fight for our equal place in the society." We all agreed.

The next year, we lost Sowmya. Unable to bear the discrimination in society, she ended her life in 2010. Eleven years have gone by and the rest of us remain unmarried. It seems only very rarely that an Indian male dares to publicly accept and acknowledge the romantic relationship with a trans woman, publicly giving her the status of a wife.

It has been more than a decade since the launch of the website. In these eleven years, we fell in love countless times, some relationships were worthy and beautiful, mostly we bit the dust with disappointments, but we still haven't lost our hopes. We believe someday, we too will have a 'prince charming moment'. Someday, a man will come into our lives, take us to his home, introduce us to his mother, and say "Ma, I love her."

What magic! It is happening now after a decade. More transwomen are marrying transmen. It is beautiful and truly magical because a transman accepts and understands a transwoman unconditionally. After all hasn't he parallelly gone through the struggles we had gone through from childhood? Even though our bodies are different, our struggles are the same. Even some transwomen are in relationship with other transwomen too. Love is Love! I accept all kinds of love.

Right now we stubbornly say 'No' to cis-gendered men who choose cowardice over acceptance, 'No' to their mother fearing made-in-India manipulations. I am still waiting for that rare gem who will break all those taboos.

Period.

The article was first published in Youth ki Awaaz in 2018. This is an updated version.

I should be
what is inside
not for what
my panty.

Known for
my head,
is inside

Arise, My Precious

My Precious,
were you driven to the street
to be the vent for
the perverts
who search for strange gutters
to duct their sperms?

Are you waiting
at the neon-lit
bypasses and
hiding in the darkness
of blind alleys
to be preyed upon
by the debauchees?

You are here to feed
the one, who in fact
belongs to the cruel crowd
that mutilated you
with its mean words
the one, who in fact
belongs to the horde

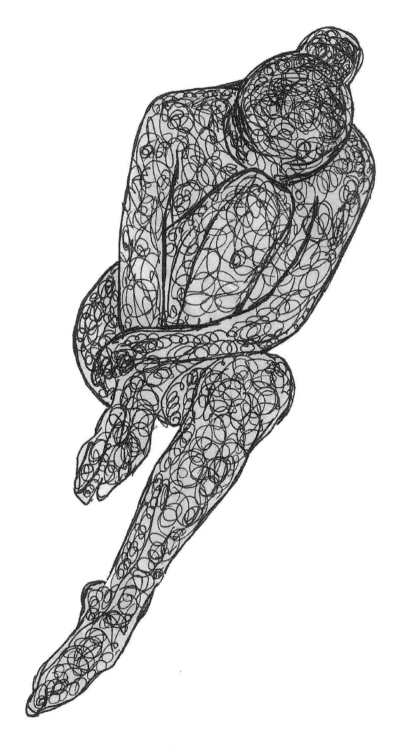

that caused the callus
in your heart
with it's heckles
and humiliating grins.

To earn your prey
alas, the irony,
you let yourself be
preyed upon first!

Why should you my dear,
though you fume with anger
to wring off the hands
which squeeze your breasts
and pluck and castaway
the penis that pulsates
to penetrate you manically,
you carry the fire embered
in your heart and
live like a walking corpse
selling your naked body
for the paper currency
printed with its price
for the 'Father of the Nation'*
fixed upon it?

---

*   *Father of the Nation (or Bapu) is how Mahatma Gandhi is fondly called by Indians. Indian currency bears his image.*

Say, how long, you propose
to disfigure yourself feeding
these morons?
what kind of life is this
to sell yourself to save your life?

Did you become a woman
for this?

Arise!
topple him off your body!
he is the agent of the insults
that strip you off your dignity,
stamp your foot on his throat
reveal your Kali-face!*
Kick at his testicles
with your scar studded
anklet-foot

Now get away from him
there is so much awaiting
to topple, battle and
get started in the world!

---

*   *Kali in Hindu mythology is a Goddess of time and death.*

May the vermilion on your forehead

scald them like the sun

and you,

my supreme creation

metamorphose as *Shakthi* incarnate[*]

Search for men who do not

peck at your heart,

search for the bliss

which does not feed on your body,

if there is ever a life firm footed

search for its roots

I too stand

in the thick of the battle field

destroying stupidity

and defeating

the emasculated,

let us celebrate life,

come.

Fear not, my precious!

Come, come my girl,

come on!

---

[*]   *Shakthi in Hindu mythology is perceived in a female form as the Primal Energy from which all entities flowed*

எழுந்திரடி என் தங்கமே

விந்தை வெளியேற்ற
வாத்தியாச இடம் தேடும்
வக்கிரக்காரர்களுக்கு
வடிகாலாய் விலைபோக
வீதிக்கு வந்துவிட்டாயோ
என் தங்கமே

சாலைகளின் சந்திப்புகளிலும்
சந்திக்காத இருட்டுகளிலும்
காசு கார்க்கு இரையாக
காத்திருக்கிறாயோ

எந்தக் இழுரர்களின்
போசச் சொற்களால்
தூரயப்படுத்தப்பட்டாயோ
எந்தக் கூட்டத்தின்
தேவலச் கிரிப்பாயும்
எக்கானத்தாயும்
உன் மணம்
காரப்புக் காய்த்ததா
அந்தக் கூபதரின்
புபி வருக்கே
இரையாக
பிரிகின்றாய்

52

தன் இரைக்காக
தான் அதிவல் இரையாகும்
அவனம் உனக்கு

உன்னிடு முலைகள் பிசையும்
அவன் கைகளையும்
உன்னை வெளியோடு
தூலைக்கத்துழுக்கும்
அவன் இளியையும்
பிய்த்து எறிகின்ற
கோபமிருந்தும்
தேசத் தந்தைக்கு
விலை வைத்த
காஇதத்தான் கழுக்கு றங்கி
நெடுப்பை வளியோடு
எருத்சில் சுமந்து
ஏனந
வெந்நூடப்பில் வாழும்
உயிர் பிணடமாய்
கிடக்கின்றாய்?

இப்பு உனை
தினம் தினம் உருக்குலைக்கும்
மிருகங்களுக்கு
இன்னும் எத்தனை நாட்கள்
இரையாவதாய் உத்தேசம்?

உன்னையே நீ
விற்று விட்டு
உயிரை மட்டும் சுமப்பது
என்ன வாழ்வு?

இதற்காகவா பெண்ணானாய்?

எழுந்திரு!
புரட்டிப்போடு அவளை
உன்னை அம்மணமாக்கும்
அவமானங்களின்
பிரதிநிதி அவன்
அவன் கழுத்தில்
கால் வைத்து உன்
காலி முகம் காட்டு!

மணிக்கெரியும் மாட்டிய
காயத்த இடுப்புகள் நிறைந்த
உன் கால்களால்
எட்டியொரு உதைபோடு
அவன் கிறிய
கிறி பார்க்கு!

புரட்டியது போதும்
அவளை
இனி புரட்டவும் போரிடவும்
நிறைய இருக்கிறது புறப்படு!

உன் நெற்றிக்கிளகம்
தூரிய னாக
உன் மொத்தழும் சக்தியின்
உஇவாக உணர்வாய்
என் உன்னைதப் படைப்பே!

மனம் கொத்தாக
டனிதரைத் தேடு!
உடல் தேடாக
உன்னைதம் தேடு!

என்றும் வீழாத
வாழ்வென்று உன்னடனில்
அதன் வேர்களைத் தேடு!

போர்க்க எத்தில் தான்
நாது மிடுக்கிஜேன்
படைமைய கொல்லு
வினைரை வென்து
வாழ்தல் கொண்டாடுவோம் வா!

பயம் கொள்ளாதே
என் துங்கமே
வாரு வா வா!

Kali, Maha Kali

Kali, Maha Kali!
you are the
unbounded Energy
Kali, Great Kali!
grant me four boons

First hand me
the wheels of time
Kali, Oh, Kali!

And then
grant me a terrifying face
to scare away mine enemies,
grant me a face with
large fiery eyes
and add to them
long canine teeth
Kali, Oh, Kali!

Grant me twenty hands
to carry all the weapons,
to strangle and slay down,

to torture and crush,
give me those twenty hands
Kali, Oh, Kali!

To embrace with childlike love
and emancipate the helpless,
give me a heart sensitive yet strong.

When you grant me these four boons
Kali, Oh Kali!
the wheel will roll back in time
to rewrite our fate afresh.

I will severe the hands
that intend to ransack our life
prior to my time and even before that
Kali, Oh, Kali!

I will garland myself
plucking heads for beads
and wear it around my neck
from where they will
dance dead on my breasts.

I will beacon the new forts
for my girls who try suicide

I rehabilitate them
to new ways of life.

I will lift them from their bed
where they are lying to die,
I will hug them and rescue them
from where they are being eaten
by the fatal worms away
their bodies they sold
for food,
Kali, Oh, Kali!

To be taken back by my parents
who chased me away,
I will stand on my toes
and cry loud as I could,
the truths to the world
that they themselves
will feel ashamed
and with aching heart run to me
and take me back.

I will restore the love and smile forever,
on the face once seemed a flower,

of the girls who carry in their eyes

the pain of love that was lost once.

If you tell me

"I gave the you boons,

now give yourself to me",

the very moment

I will return to you

and surrender my life at your feet.

Kali, Oh, Kali*

grant me four boons!

You are the

unbounded energy

Great Kali, please do!

---

*   *Kali in Hinduism is the goddess of death and time, the destroyer of evil.*

வரம் கொடு

காளி மகாகாளி
எல்லையற்ற
மகாசக்தியே !
நான்கு வரங்கள்
கொடு எனக்கு.

முதலில்
தாலச்சக்கரத்தை
கையில் கொடு

அகன்ற அகன்ற அக்னி விழிகளும்
கீண்ட கோரைப் பற்களுமாய்
பகைவர் அச்சும்
பயங்கர முகம் கொடு

இழுக்கவும், அறுக்கவும்
வதைக்கவும் சிதைக்கவும்
ஆயுதங்கள் தாங்கிய
இருபது கைகள் கொடு

அன்போடு தழுவும்
இழந்தை மழையும்
ஆழ்ந்தகன்ற அகன்றும்
வல்லமை இணையும்
ஒன்றாய் கொண்ட
இதயம் கொடு

நானிரு வரங்கள்
தாரே நீ தந்தயின்
விதியினை மாற்றி
புதியதை எழுதவே
காலச் சக்கரத்தை
சுழற்றிச் சுழற்றிச்
செல்வேன் பின்னே

எனக்கு முன்யும்
அதற்கு முன்யும்
எம்மை
அடைமயாட விழைந்த
இயவர்களின் தைத்தை
கதறக்கதற
அறுப்பேன்

எம் உயிர்பலிா
எம் உயர்பலிக்க
எத்தனித்த வெளியர்களின்
தலைகளை
கொய்து கொய்து
மாலைகளாய்
கோர்த்துக் கோர்த்து
மாலைகளின்
மார்பின்மேல்
அட அட
தவழவிடுவேன்

அனைத்தையும்
இழந்ததாய்
தந் நேரகாலைகளில்
உயிர் இழுக்க
எத்தனித்த எம்மக்கள்
விதியினை மாற்றி
வாழ்வைத் தருும்
வழிகளை காட்டுவேன்

வயிற்றுப் பசிக்கு
உடலை விற்று
உயிர்க் கொள்ளிகளை
உள்ளுக்குள் வாங்கி
மரணப் படுக்கையில்
மரத்துக் கிடப்போரை
மார்போடு அனைத்து
மீட்டெடுப்பேன்

எம்மைத் துரத்திய
அம்மையும் அப்பனும்
உணர்வுகள் புரிந்து
வேதனையில் வெட்கித்து
ஓடோடி வந்து எம்மை
அணைத்துக் செல்லவே
உரத்து உரத்து
ஓலமிட்டு உண்மைகளை
உலகிக்குச் சொல்வேன்

காதலால் கருதி
காயக்கள் புறையோட
வலிகளை மட்டுமே
வழிகளில் சுமந்த
நடைதையரின் வாழ்வதனில்
நிலைத்து நின்றிடும்
புதிய காதலையும்
~~பூமித்தின்~~ பூமிகத்தில் புன்னகையையும்
நிரந்தரமாக்கித் தருவேன்

வரங்கள் தந்தேன்
கேட்டபடி நானுக்கு
உன்னைக் கொடு
இக்கணமே எனக்கு
என்று என் தாபே
என்னை நீ கேட்பாயெனில்
அக்கணமே
உன் காவலயில் விழுந்து
எனதுயிரை உனதாக்குவேன்

தாயே மகாகாளி
இக்கணமே
இப்பொழிதே
நான்கு வரங்கள்
கொடு எனக்கு.

Sexual violence

horrible, health

that transgender

endured for

is a terrible,

affecting issue

people have

over a Century.

A Mutilated Vagina Called Eezham[*]

After
the blood I shed
dried up,
the scars carved
on my vagina
still remain
as my identity.

Nowadays
when I touch
those scars,
Oh,
I am scalded
by the memories
of my sister in Eelam
who died,
with her stomach torn
and
her vagina wailing
agape.

---

[*]   *Eezham is the name of the freedom land the Tamil liberals fought for in Srilanka*

I,

on my quest for self,

and she,

on her exodus for Eezham,

we

both bore the pain.

Oh,

I know

her agony

And I know

the odour and wetness

of her dripping blood.

As I have gone

to the threshold

of her pain,

now I feel closer

to her.

The beasts that

tore her open,

did not stop with

killing her.

Oh, they also

smashed on the ground

the heads of her
little ones.

Oh…Oh…Oh,
the beasts are still
alive and prowling
around.
What shall I do?

Oh
the stray dogs who
sneer at me
as I am transgender,

and bear the semblance
of those beasts
who mauled my sister
to death.

When injustice is
inflicted upon me,
at once
the snarling tiger
in me wakes up,
fuming with wrath.
My eyes grow

fiercely red

and my veins

throb with anger.

Oh,

when the same injustice

is inflicted upon my race,

where are those

fierce eyes?

Where are those

throbbing veins?

Where did my

historic valour

of Thamizh woman go?

Oh,

they deceived me

with their fictions!

Oh, my Thamizh,

what have you taught me

other than

unpremeditated

recital of poetry

and

bemoaning with my

head bowed?

Oh,

you put my

entire generation

into

incurable intoxication!

Oh,

the scars of humiliation

given by my identity

are still on my heart.

The graves of those

missing Thamizhs,

the sad history of

the Eezham lost,

are buried

in the tracks of tears

shed by my

reddened eyes.

And the agony and scars

of my Tamil race

are buried in my

withered and mutilated

vagina.

ஈ-யும் என்றொரு கிழிந்த யோனி

நான் கிந்திய ஒருதி
காய்ந்த பின்
செதுக்கிய வடுக்கள்
அடையாளங்களாக
என் யோனியால்
நிலைக்கின்றன

இப்பொழுதெல்லாம்
வடுக்களை நான் தொடும்போது
ஐயோ
வயிறு கிழிழந்து யோனி பிழந்து பிறந்து
இறந்து போன
என் ஈ.ழுத்த கோதரியின்
நினைவுகள்
நெருப்பாய் தகிக்கிறதே

எனக்கான தேடலில் நானும்
தன் இனத்திற்கான தேடலில்
அவளும் எவளும்
வலி சுமந்தோரே !
அவள் வலியால்
செரிப்ப வலியும்
வழிந்த ஒருதியின்
வாசமும் ஈ.ரமும்
நானறி வேனே

75

அந்த வலயின் வாசல்வரை
சென்று வந்தேன் என்பதாலேயே
அவருக்கு நான்
இன்னும் நெகிழ்த்தடாளேனே

அவளை பிறந்து
தொன்ற மிருகங்கள்
அத்தோடு விடவில்லையே
அவள் பெற்ற நன்மத்தனையும்
துறையில் தலையடித்துக் கொன்றதரே

ஓலோ அப்பாடு கங்கள்
இன்னும் உயிருடன்
உலவிக்கொண்டதானே இருக்கின்ற
என் தெய்வேன் ?

திருநங்கை எனைக்கண்டு
சிரிக்கும் தெருநாய் களிடம்
அவளை சிதைத்துக்கொன்ற
மிருகங்களின் சாயலைக்
காண்கிறேன்
விறுவிறுவென்று
வெறிகொண்ட
வேங்கை ஒன்று
உள்ளே திடுக்கென்று
விழிக்கிறது

எனக்கான ஒன்று
நடக்கிம்போது
விழி சிவந்து
நரம்புகள் புடைக்கின்றதே
என் இனத்திற்கான
ஒன்று நடக்கிம்போது
ஏன் சிவக்கவில்லை
புடைக்கவில்லை?
எங்கே போயிற்று
தமிழச்சி என்
வரலாற்று வீரம்?

ஐயோ
புனைவுக்கதைகள் சொல்லி
எனை ஏமாற்றிவிட்டனரே?

தமிழே
தனை மறந்து
கவிதை சொல்வதையும்
தலை கவிழ்ந்து
கவலை கொள்வதையும் தவிர
வேறென்ன கற்றுக் கொடுத்தாய்
எனக்கு?
என் தலைமுறையையே
மயக்கத்தில்
வைத்தாயே?

ஐயோ
என் அடையாளம்
தந்த அவமானங்கள்
இதயத்தில்
கீறல்களாய் இருக்க,

தொலைந்த தமிழரின்
சுவக்கு மிக ரும்
இழந்த எ·ழத்தின்
வரலாறு களும்
சிவந்த என் விழிகளில்
வழிந்த கண்ணீர் தோடுகளிலும்
சிதைந்த என் யோனியின்
காய்ந்த மேடுகளிலும்
இறந்த என் இனத்தின்
வலிகளும்
வடுக்களுடாய்
புதைந்து போயினவே ....

Piece by Piece

I am not a woman by birth
I was born as a shattered
Rubik's cube,
all my life I worked
step by step
to reclaim my honour.

To correct the wrongs,
I collected all of me,
my body, mind and soul
and put them together in patience,
vouching with perseverance.
I endured shame and guilt,
yet I stood strong with grit.

This person that
you see as me,
she wrote her own life script.
With a rose and a smile,
she ran mile after mile,
from pillars to posts,

to prove her dignity

and gain respect.

She no more fears,

and doesn't do tears.

Farewell to the boy who was She,

Welcome to the joy for all new Me.

Some fathers
menstruate
and
Some mothers
can't
breast feed.

The Story of Two

I was fourteen
when I heard this story
from my *Thirunangai* *amma*.
A story of two,
a love that was true,
hidden from the world
but told to a few.

He was born she,
she was born he,
they both fled
from the fangs of
their families
to have a life
of their own.
Free to live
free to love.

Then one day
his family found him,

and ripped him away.
Their pleading tears
and grieving screams
were cruelly slammed.

Trapped by the
vengeful clutches
of false pride,
he was abducted
and taken
to be a bride.

Robbed of clothes and
saree forcedly draped,
night and day
he was mercilessly raped.
A string of yellow thread
was all that entitled
his life to be scrapped.

He got pregnant
and tried to end his life,
hearing his fate
she slit herself with a knife.

Crushed into
a million pieces
when he heard,
deep inside his core
he was a dead bird,
memories of her
beautiful face were
all that remained.

He carried a stranger
within his womb,
who twisted endless
sorrow and gloom.

He ran away
to another town,
in hunger to survive
he sold himself
and let his health down.

Fate never smiled
but only frowned,
AIDS took him down
and in drugs he drowned.

Unable to bear

and sheltered nowhere,

he died on the streets

no one to care.

When I heard the story, I wept several nights for him and for her, I still do. They remain victims of the sick patriarchy, of cultural policing, of homophobia and transphobia. How many other stories are buried, are forgotten and remain untold?

Clap Aloud

Clap aloud
Thirunangai
clap aloud!
Like a crack of thunder
that shocks the world
during a great rain,
clap your hands aloud!

Until the ray of light
streaks across
the dark hearts
of those off-springs
who run after money
in a rat- race
tossing their elders
in old-age homes,
raise your hands

and clap aloud
my Thirunangai
clap aloud!

They forget their
mother tongue
and proudly speak
another language,
to make them bow
their head in shame
and spread Thamizh fast
like the power of flame,
your clap should prod them
Clap, girl clap!

The foolishness
of the fanatics
who subjugate women
in the name of religion,

clap your hand

clap, clap, clap

to cry aloud

'Down! Down! Down!'

the culture cops

'Down! Down! Down!'

Drum a drum!

Drum a drum, my girl!

The greedy ones,

who cheat the poor farmers

and rob them of their only lands

to build multi-stories

in the tiller's soil

and sell them

for a price so high,

till their ear drums

tear off and hang out

below their ear lobes,

clap aloud,

Thirunangai clap aloud!

These hands,

my Thirunangai,

these hands

that clapped

for money till now,

these hands Thirunangai

these hands,

that clapped to ignite the fire,

to burn the heckles and mocking,

these hands, my Thirunangai

these hands,

that clapped in rhythm of joy

and clapped in happy festivity,

hereafter

may these hands open

books to build new heaven,

may crack the whip

to strip injustice naked

and may these hands,

my Thirunanagai

these hands,

join the palms to accept

the honour garlanded

on grand occasions

of learned gatherings.

ஓங்கிக் கை தட்டு
~~ஓங்கிக்கை~~
திரு நங்கையே!
பெரு மழையான் போது
உலகுக்கின்ற பேரிடிபோல்
பூமி அதிர அதிர
ஓங்கித்தட்டு
உன் கைகளை!

பொற்றோடை
முதியோர் இல்லத்தில்
கண்ணீரில் தள்ளிவிட்டு
காண்பதற்கு நேரமின்றி
காசு பண்ண அலையும்
இரக்கமற்ற பிள்ளைகளின்
இருண்ட இதயங்களில்
வெளிச்சக்கீற்று
விழும்வரை
ஓங்கி ஓங்கித்தட்டு
உன் கைகளை!

தாய்மொழியை
மறந்து விட்டு
அயல்மொழியை
அருமை மொழியாய்
எண்ணி
பெருமையாய் கற்கும்
அறிகற்றோர் அனைவரும்

வெடித் தலைகீ நிந்து
வேகமாய் தமிழ்கற்க
ஆங்கித்தட்டு
உன் கைகளை

மதங்களின் பெயரால்
பெண்களை
அழுமை கொள்ளும்
மனம் இருண்ட
கலாச்சார காவலர்களின்
மடமை ஒழிக
ஒழிக ஒழிக வென்று
ஆங்கி ஆங்கித்தட்டு
உன் கைகளை!

ஊர்உமுத நிலங்களை
ஏமாற்றி வாங்கிக்கொண்டு
பண்ணடுக்கு வீடுகட்டி
கூறுபோட்டு
கூலிவிற்கும்
பெருமுத லாளிகளின்
ஆசிப்பனை கிழிந்து
தொங்கும்வரை
ஆங்கி ஆங்கித்தட்டு
உன் கைகளை!

இதுவரை கைதட்டி

நடிக்காக கைவேந்திய
இக்கைகள்
கேலியை கிண்டலை
நெடுப்பாக சுட்டெறிந்த
ஆங்காரமை இப்பிய
இக்கைகள்

மகிழ்ச்சியிலும் இலவியிலும்
கூப்பாடு போட்ட
இக்கைகள்

இனி புத்தகங்கள்
திறந்து புதுவுலகம்
சமைக்கட்டும் !

அநீதிகளை அம்மணமாக்கி
சவுக்கடி கொடுக்கட்டும் !

மாபெரும் சபைகளில்
மாமனிதர் நடுவிகில்
தோள்களில் மாலைபோடு
கைதடப்பி வணைத்தட்டும் !

It doesn't

Son is a

your daughter

really matters

you are as a

matter if your daughter, or is a Son. What is how good father or mother.

A Letter to a Transgender Kid

Hello Darling,

Listen. It is amazing that you have this opportunity to read my letter to you. I write this to you from India, a land of diversity and rich cultural heritage. India is the spiritual capital of the world, true knowledge and wisdom has always been born here and has enlightened human kind for thousands of years. I believe I have a handful of drops from this great land. I give a drop of that knowledge from the ocean of wisdom.

You sure know the power of human thought. Our thoughts make up our actions and our actions make up our life. You are what you think. You are the sum of your thoughts. Your thoughts design your destiny. At this point of your life, you are here reading this because you DECIDED to read this. That decision is your thought.

We are trans and we are special. This road ahead of you will be filled with roses and thorns. Sometimes with less roses and more thorns. If you stamp on the thorns and fall, remove them from your feet, stand up and keep walking. Life is a journey, when we stop there is no meaning. Keep moving.

The first thing I want you to do is respect and love yourself. Nowhere in your journey should you self-pity, devalue, underestimate or hurt yourself. Stand tall. You are special, you are unique in the entire universe, believe me there is only one as YOU. As a creation you are already complete. You strive to change your form through transition which is truly your own identity. Do it wisely. Plan your life ahead. There is no rush. Give enough time. That is very important.

Research and find the right information about your gender identity. There are many online tests on gender, go for them. Find an experienced and understanding doctor to help you. Know your body well. If you decide to take hormone therapy, try to go for natural supplements rather than synthetic ones.

Smile at people, make friends, and help them. There are so many nice people out there who understand you, accept you as you are and will support you in your transition. My friends have been my biggest strength. During my transition and after that, they took the responsibility of healing me. I owe to them lifelong; I can never stand equal in their sacrifices and selfless love for me. I have abundance of gratitude for them. Choose your friends and keep them forever.

Fall in love. If that love fails you, don't fall down. Don't lose heart. Keep going. It is so much important to love yourself and move on. Let love find you. Don't be desperate.

Do remember that there is no complete man or complete women in this world. If anyone as such existed ever, they can never understand the emotions of the opposite gender. In every man, there is a woman and, in every woman, there is a man. How much of a man is a woman, and how much of a woman is a man is what makes them. Makes us all.

Through these words, I give you more courage and love, I give you the strength to take wise decisions in your life, I wish you all good luck and success.

Lovingly,

– **Kalki Subramaniam**

Nirvaanam*

The brand-new anklet
gifted by my *Gurubhai***
scintillatingly complained
from my legs,

with heart's joy brimmed
onto my lips
I hummed a tune
skipped a foot
and
fluttered like a butterfly.

"There goes the *pottai****"*
heckled those
who have their manhoods
hanging about them,

---

*   *Nirvaanam or Nirvaan is the eternal liberation, the process of sex reassignment surgery or castration (as called by sections of transgender people).*
**   *Gurubhai is a sister of a thirunangai from the transgender family*
***   *Pottai is a derogatory word in Thamizh used to degrade a person as impotent or blind*

abruptly
died my smile,
I perspire all over,
the nerves pervading
all over my body
feel the parching fire,
I gnash my teeth
my furtive finger nails
throb to transform
themselves in to maces.

My wrath rises
to pounce like a tigress
on those morons,
tear their stomach
and draw out their bowels.

My anger changing
in to curses
charged upon them,
the saree head slipped
I stood half naked.

Then one of them hollered
"What a shame
you call yourself a woman?
you stand in front of us
slipping your saree?"

My eyes reddened

and veins throbbed,

I stand my ground

to prove my womanhood,

with tears rolling down

I remove my saree.

In this moment,

I do not want any *Krishna*[*]

to save or rescue me

like he who in the royal court

saved the esteem

of Draupadi

by giving her a saree.

"See me

you wretched whore's son

I am not a man

I AM A WOMAN"

I beat my hands

ferociously on my femininity.

---

*   *Krishna in the Indian epic Mahabharata is the reincarnation of Vishnu. When Kauravas, the rivals of Pandavas strip Draupadi, the Pandava queen whom her husband have pawned and lost in a game of dice, she cries for the help of Lord Krishna and the invisible God protects for with an unlimited length of saree that the Kauravas are not able to strip her naked in the royal court.*

நிர்வாணம்

என் இருபால்
புதிதாய் பரிசனித்த
கோயுகிகள்
என் காலல் கினுங்கின

உள்ளத்தில் மகிழ்ச்சி
உதயில் பொங்க
பாடிக்கதாண்டே
பட்டாம் பூச்சியை
பறக்கின்றேன்
நடக்கின்றேன்

" போகிறது யார் பொட்டை "
என்று நகைத்துச் சிரித்தார்கள்
ஆண்டையை
தொங்க விட்டுக் கொண்டிருப்பவர்கள்

தட்டென்று கசத்துப் போனது
என் புன்னகை
விறுவிறு வென்று
வோர்க்கின்றது எனக்கு
உடல் மிருக்க
கிளை விரித்த
நரம்புகளினலல்லாம்
தடுப்பேற

நுர்நுர்வென்று
பற்கலை
பற்கலை தழுக்கிறேன்
பரபரக்கும்
என் விரல்கங்கள்
வேல்களாக
மாறத் துடிக்கின்றன

அந்பர்கள் மீது
புளியாய் பாய்ந்து
வயிறு கிழித்து
இடல் உருவ
வெளி எறுகிறது

கோபங்கள் சாபங்களாய்
சிறிச்சிறி அவர்கள் மேல்
விழுந்தன
அறை நிர்வாணமானேன்

அப்போது ஒருவன்
"ஏண்டா பொம்பளாயாடா நீ?
சேலையை அவுத்துப்டு நிக்கற"
என்றான்

அன்று சபையினர் ஒன்பு
பெண்மையின் மானம் காக்க
சேலை கொடுத்தான் கண்ணன்

114

இப்போது அவன்
எனக்கு வேண்டாம்

இன்று
என் பெண்மையை
நிரூபித்து
மானம் ~~தாங்~~ காக்க
கண்ணீருடன்
என் சேலையை
நானே அவிழ்க்கிறேன்

"பாடுடா
கண்டாரு .... மைவனே
நான் ஆம்பள
இல்லடா
பொம்பள"
ஓங்கி ஓங்கி
தைக்களை அழுத்தேன்
வைதியோடு.

I am a
woman and I
That doesn't
Woman? My
old and doesn't
either. She is not a

transgender

don't menstruate.

mean I am not a

mother is 65 years

menstruate

woman anymore?

Truth and Lie

After he left,
I stumbled and gathered
my own broken pieces,
thinking to myself
why can't this moment
of rejection be
just a nightmare
from which I could wake up?

My eyes were streaming
with the burning tears,
which I couldn't control
and didn't want to.
I didn't have the strength
to wipe them away either,
But I knew, I would be okay
when he was gone far away.

"I told you not to out
yourself as a Transwoman.
My parents rejected you,
I need them and
can't reject them,

so I reject you"
you spoke.

You! before you leave
know that
my courage has
outed your cowardice.
Good for me that
I know you now.
Get the hell out of my life,
I would rather live with
the truth and die
than live with you as a lie.

I am broken yes,
but I will be fine.
I am a strong person,
I have learned to
build myself back.

Maybe it will take
sometime to
get rid of your shadow,
but life will flow
and I will shine.

My Perfectly Imperfect Vagina

It took half a lifetime for me to have a vagina. Really half of my life time. I have always wanted to have one, a perfect one like born women and like some of our trans girls had. Women who are 'born women' are gifted with a perfect vagina, they don't have to spend a dime or a rupee to have a perfect one.

But our stories, the transwomen's stories are entirely different. Before we did our sex reassignment surgeries, those days whenever we looked down naked, we were ashamed and wanted to pluck it off whatever was hanging there. We loathed it.

The evenings I and my girly girls were together, we always spoke about our future vaginas. Or talk about someone who recently had a new vagina by paying a hefty amount to a quack doctor. We all know he was a quack, but we still envied as well as marvelled at her decision to go under the knife. Like many of my friends, I had to wait many years to get the gift. Those sad and insecure days, I felt awfully bad. My body felt horribly wrong.

After many years of desperation, and many thousand voices like mine began to raise for our rights, we were finally heard. For the first time, the government had compassion for us. We were lucky. A special ward in the state's capital was opened for us. Doctors began to do free sex reassignment surgeries.

So, one by one, me and many of my friends went happily to the operation theatres to be transformed, the get rid of what we didn't wanted and embrace the gift we had been waiting all of our lives for.

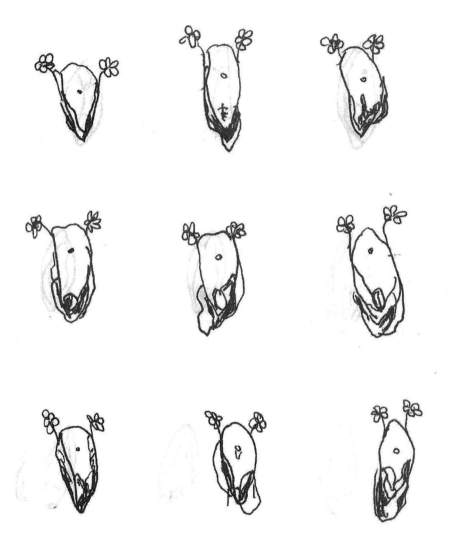

We trusted the doctors and believed in them. They gave promises which lighted up our faces and heart. At that time, they looked like Gods, the angels who can transform us. Ah… but we didn't know we were the specimens for their learning process.

You know, none of them had prior experience in doing sex reassignment surgeries, yet they promised us that we will have perfect vaginas like those girls who went to Bangkok hospitals and had it. We had no choice, all we had was so much hope. What else can we have when we don't have money? We all agreed to the surgeries because we were all desperate for a vagina and had no money.

We were given dates for our surgeries, our hearts pounded and we were anxious. Usually on each of the specified dates, two surgeries were performed. After our surgeries, we were put next to each other in beds. Once in every two weeks, new surgeries were performed and the old patients will empty the beds.

It started slowly. The realization. When our bandages were removed in the hospital, we all began to check our vaginas. To our amazement, astonishment and embarrassment, each of our vaginas looked different. You don't understand what I am saying. Many didn't look like a vagina at all. We thought probably because of the swelling it looked disfigured.

Then the opinions, complaints and annoyance started. Each vagina was different, yes but different totally. Some girls had great difficulty in urinating, some had a small hole drilled for sexual intercourse, some had a hole that was just two inches, for some it was three inches. Many vaginas were loose and hanging. We understood that our vaginas will be disqualified for intercourse.

Our labia were other episodes and chapters of hysteria. It was all improper and a big joke played on us. For many, it looked out of shape, extra skin hanging loose, wrinkled and ugly. It didn't take much time for us to realise the first batch of us were all the lab rats on whom they experimented their skills on.

That is how those idiots or should I call them smart doctors learned to do sex reassignment surgeries. They still do, but I heard they make better vaginas these days.

As for my vagina, it is only three inches deep and with much difficulty and some great tricks it could qualify for intercourse. But no, I am not interested in sex anymore and so the shape of my vagina doesn't really matter to me anymore. I want to get rid of what I didn't want, and I got rid of it. That's all that matters to me. I guess it is not the same with the other girls. Well, they have their own vagina stories and monologues.

You see, we don't talk about vaginas with the public, especially our own. So I think you have minimum luck. Maybe you should wait for them to talk about it. If at all I get to meet those doctors in my life again (I heard one is already dead), I would kick their balls till they faint in pain. That I certainly will do.

Empowered

Empower

Transwomen

Transwomen.

Ravens

The ravens on the neem tree
looked at the little boy,
sitting down below
sobbing and wailing.

They felt sorry for the kid
who was sharing his food
generously with them
whenever he would come.

He visited the park
often these days,
he was lonely and sad
long hours he stayed.

Buried in his palms
and sobbing in sadness
was his beautiful face,
the ravens heard him say
"Why me, why me?"

When no one around

he spoke to the ravens,

"I feel this way

I tell this to you,

I don't want

to be a man,

what can I do?".

Phallus, I Cut

No Transcendental Yoga
I performed
To transform myself
In to a woman.

I cut my phallus,
soiled in blood
and transcending death
I became a woman.

"Oh, you do not have
ovary,
woman, you are not."
said you.
Well.

"Ay, wait!
as you have severed
your manhood,
you are now
a desolate tree with
decayed barks,

you have dug
the grave of
your own lineage,
live, you may
till your roots last,
the earth that bears you
shall give up
one day
as you have not
planted your branches
below."
said, you.

Well.

I do not want an ovary
to carry your excretions
of caste and religious
fanaticism.

And I do not want
in my ovary
the gestation of
those seeds
to grow in to a
tyrannous tree.

Many a woman
as she carried
the seeds of your
discriminations,
made her ovary
your lavatory.

Luckily,
I am not a woman
by birth,
and that you refuse
to accept me as one
is, in fact,
my real freedom.
I do not recite
the gyno-grammar
you have crafted.

call me
an error of nature,
call me what you will,
I know it myself
for sure
who I am
at any given hour.

Renouncing religion,

casting away caste,

we are united

as the rejected.

can you live

this life we live?

can you become a mother

without carrying a womb?

can you become a daughter

without sucking at

your mother's breast?

I can.

Cut the phallus

of your chauvinism

and then you will know

who you are,

and then,

and only then,

you tell me

that

I am not a woman.

குறி அறுத்தேன்

மாதவம் எதும்
செய்யவில்லை நான்
குறி அறுத்து
குருதியில் நனைந்து
மரணம் கடந்து
மங்கையானேன்
கருவறை உனக்கில்லை
நீ பெண்ணில்லை என்றீர்கள்
நல்லது

ஆண்டமையை அறுத்ததிந்ததால்
சந்ததிக்கு சமாதி கட்டிய
பட்டுப்போன ஒற்றைமரம் நீ,
விடுதுதள் இல்லை உனக்கு
வேர்கள் உள்ளவரை மட்டுமே
பூமி உனை தாங்கும்
என்றீர்கள்
நல்லது

நீங்கள் குழிக்கும்
எச்சங்களை
சாதி வெறியும் மதவெறியும் கொண்டு
நீங்கள் விருட்சமாக்க
விதை போட்ட உங்கள்
மிச்சங்களை
சிசுவாக சுமக்கிற

கருவறை எனக்கு வேண்டாம்
உங்கள் ஏற்றத்தாழ்வு
எச்சங்களை சுமந்தால்
பாவம்
அவள் கருவறை
கழிவறை ஆனது

நல்லவேளை
பிறப்பால் நான் பெண்ணில்லை
என்னை பெண்ணாக
நீங்கள் ஏற்க மறுத்ததே
எனக்குக் கிடைத்த விடுதலை

பெண்மைக்கு
நீங்கள் வகுத்துள்ள
அழகு இலக்கணங்களை
நான் வாசிப்பதில்லை
என்னை இயற்கையின் பிழை
என்று தாராளமாய்
சொல்லிக்கொள்ளுங்கள்
நான் யார் என்பதை
நானே அறிவேன்

மதம் மறந்து சாதி துறந்து
மறுக்கப்பட்டவங்கள்
ஒன்றுகூடி
வாழும் வாழ்க்கையை

141

வாழ முடியுமா உங்களால்?

கருவில் சாமக்காமலேயே
தாயாக முடியுமா உங்களால்?

மார் முட்டிப் பசியாறு மகவேயே
மகனாக முடியுமா
உங்களால்?

என்னால் முடியும்

உங்களின் ஆணாதிக்க
குறியை அறுத்துக் கொள்ளுங்கள்
நீங்கள் யார் என்பதை
அப்போது
நீங்கள் அறிவீர்கள்

பிறகி சொல்லுங்கள்
நான் பெண்ணில்லை என்று.

Half a Woman

"Di, do you know to cook?"
"I don't know Gurubhai."

"Di, can you draw *kolam**?"
"Don't know how."

"*Kothi***, what do you know then?"

I laugh.

"A sari looks beautiful on you
than a t-shirt and jeans,
wear it di."

"I don't know how to wrap a sari, *gurubhai*"!

"You don't know anything…
What do you know ha…

---

*   *Kolam is beautiful and intrinsic patterns drawn around multiple dots carefully laid on the front yards of Indian households every morning. There are thousands of designs and patterns available which traditionally women are to learn from their young age.*

**   *Kothi is used by transgender community in slang or fondly to call each other.*

143

I'm not your brother.
I'm not your son.
I'm not your nephew.
I'm not him.
Don't call me he.

I am your SISTER.
I am Your DAUGHTER.
I am your NIECE.
I am HER.
Call me SHE.

you call yourself a woman!"
Laughed my gurubhai fondly.

If this and this
is what strictly
defines me as a woman,
then I am not one.
I shall remain half a woman.

We don't need

proclaim to

we are

a title to

the world that

beautiful. ✓

Fate, I Wrote

Wedded to God,

widowed in a day,

I am an experimental poem,

my nuptial knot

stayed firm and fast

just from dawn to dusk.

After that, around a tree,

was wound

my wedding thread*

and I learned

the threadbare string

will dry

and dissolve into dust.

---

*   Thousands of transgender women visit the Koothandavar temple in Kuvagam
village in Tamilnadu every year during Chitra Pournami (full moon) and perform
the ceremony of marrying God Koothandavar also known as prince Aravaan.
After dancing, singing and celebrating all night, the next day their Thaali (yellow
thread) is cut of, bangles broken and the Kungumam wiped off to embrace
windowhood.
The legend says Krishna took the form of a woman, Mohini and married prince
Aravan. When he was sacrificed to Kali to win the war, Mohini embraces widowhood
and does the mourning ceremonies. Many transgender women believe they are
incarnations of Krishna as Mohini and perform the ceremony in the Koothandavar
temple.

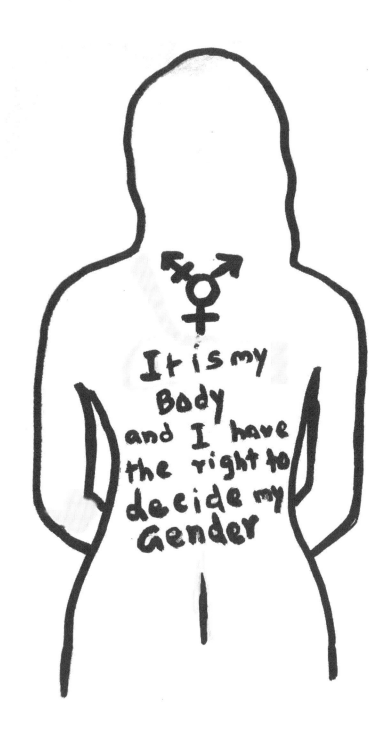

It will not, ever,

never ever

decide even my life's crust.

All of you,

have your horoscope

divined by celestial rite.

But for me,

by my will to right,

mine, I can as well write.

My knowledge tells,

"The string makes no sense.

Just a severed yellow thread.

This it is and nothing else."

As I abhorred the ordeal,

I dumped it in a gutter.

And I decided

to wear forever,

a smile that

serenades the living hour.

And I familiarised

myself with the

fervent language of the

flower.

And I learned avidly,

the liberal art of limitless

loving.

And now I know,

my dear, dear friend,

how to live precisely,

like poetry.

விதியை எழுதினேன்

கடவுளுக்கு மனைவியாகி
ஒருநாளில் அதிக விதவையான
ஒரு பரிசோதனை
கவிதை நான்,
என் தாலியும் வாழ்வு
ஒருநாள் மட்டும்.

அறுத்த என் தாலி
எங்கோ மரத்தில் கட்டுப்பட்டு
மக்கிப்போய் மண்ணாகியிருக்கும்,
அந்தத் தாலி
என் விதியை நிர்ணயிப் பதில்லை
என்பதை அறிந்துகொண்டேன்

எல்லோருக்கும் ஜாதகம்
இருக்கும்
எனக்கு இல்லை,
என் விதியை
நானே எழுதிக்கொள்ள
~~என~~ எனக்கிருக்கிறது
வலிமை மிக்க ஒரு மனம்
தெளிவு பெற்ற என் அறிவு

அறுத்தெறிந்த தாலிக்கு
அர்த்த மில்லை

வெறும் டஞ்சன் கயிறு
அதில் ஒன்றுமில்லை
அந்த வேதனைச் சடங்கு
எனக்கு வேண்டாம்

சடங்குகளை ஒட்டைகட்டி
சாத்தடைக்குள் போட்டபின்
புன்னகை செய்ய கற்றுக்கொண்டேன்
பூக்களோடு பேச கற்றுக்கொண்டேன்
காதலுக்க கற்றுக்கெண்டேன்
கவிதை எழுத கற்றுக்கொண்டேன்
கவிதையாகவே வாழவும்
இன்று கற்றுக்கொண்டேன்.

The Future is Non-Binary

The future is the expansion of gender and sexuality. The future is non-binary. It truly is.

What has become of transgender people now will see a revolutionary change in the next 25 years. In 2050, Transgender people will matter, their contributions will matter not only for the country they live in, but for the entire world. One of the greatest discoveries in science will be by a transgender person.

Countries will be still with borders, but the collective consciousness of people worldwide will become one large community of humans who will began to see beyond borders, respecting and accepting each other. Within the large sphere of the human race will be each community unearthing its own roots and beginnings, finding the hidden knowledge of their respective ancestors, their wisdom in science, technology, medicine, astronomy and spirituality. In 2050, we will look back at ourselves and be ashamed of how much of a casteist, racist and fundamentalist we had been. How we were divided by the color of skin and the languages we spoke? We will be ashamed of how much money we had spent on war but ignored the poor. Does it all sound like a distant utopian dream or just an impossibility?

In the future, we will realise that diversity in gender and sexuality is natural and there has been much injustice done to homosexual and transexual population over holding onto centuries of outdated law across the world. Gender justice will prevail, men, women, transgender people and non-binary will be treated equally and enjoy their rights.

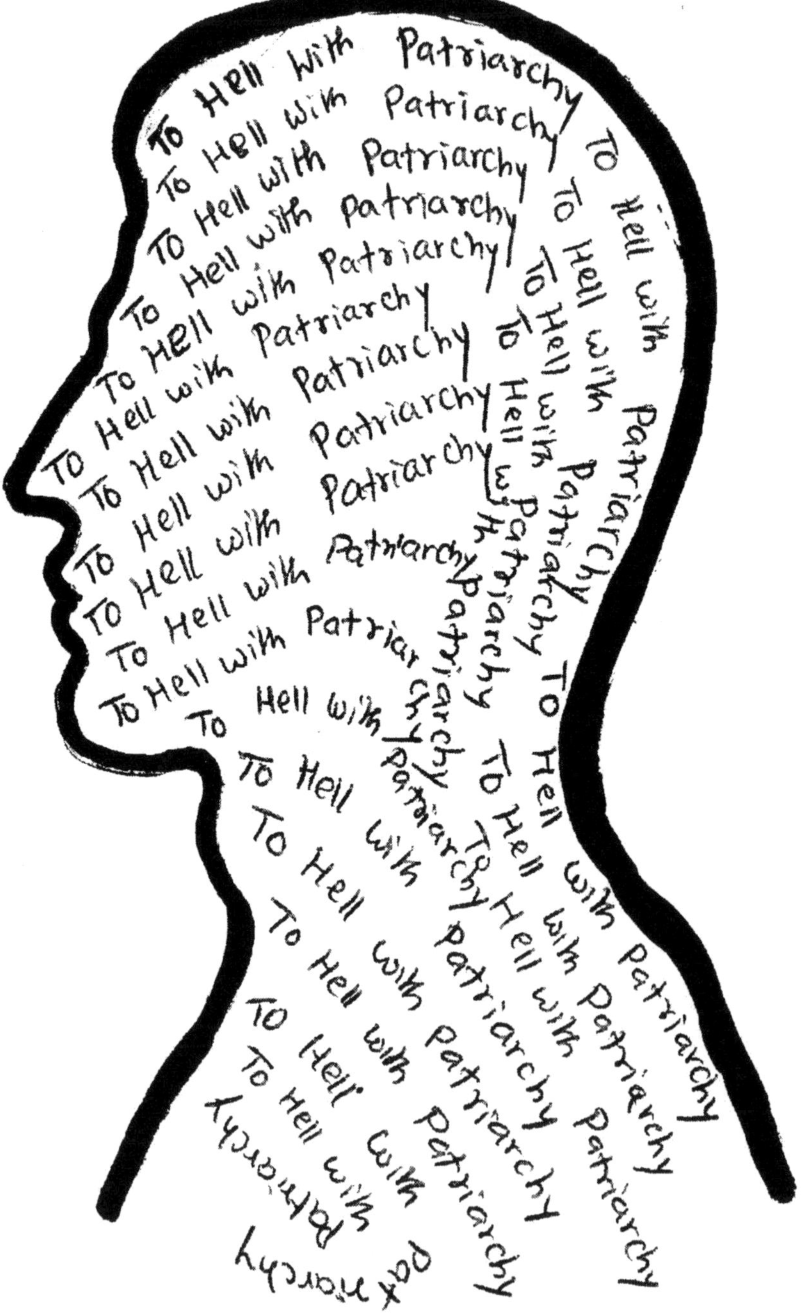

The future belongs to those who embrace each other and acknowledge our presence. In contemporary Indian society, the identities beyond the binary of male and female is still looked upon as a taboo, at least in fashion to some extend it may be not be but otherwise the stereotypes are so strong it stinks how we still refuse to acknowledge that it is okay to be gay or a trans. The future will belong to those who contribute to the intellectual, spiritual and spiritual consciousness of the humanity. LGBTQIA+ people will be in the centre of that making this world a more meaningful and beautiful place.

In 2050, the then Indian youth will read about how transgender people were stigmatised and were exploited for more than 200 years and they will make sure that mistake never happens ever again. Transgender individuals will not be begging anymore, nor will they be standing on roads for sex work. That will be an ignorant previous generation's horrible crime against the transgender community. It will be regretted.

2050 will begin the light years for the transgender community, there will be transgender people who will own massive corporations, will be influential leaders and politicians, will sweep the world with the charm and art, will lead in education, science and research. Our environment will have changed drastically but we will find a way to survive. Medical miracles will happen and be discovered by transgender individuals.

Marriage will be a new meaningful union without any strains for LGBTQIA+ people. Across many countries all over the world, LGBTQIA+ leaders will unite to develop new strategies to keep this world more peaceful. Transgender astronomers will fly to Mars or someone who had travelled to Mars to out himself/herself as trans. True love will blossom and love of all kinds will be accepted.

India will be the heartbeat of spiritual knowledge more than ever; it will also be the heartland for the Transgender people all over the world. A great leader for the people of the entire world will emerge from the LGBTQI community.

Does whatever I say sound like an imaginary utopian wish or a distance dream or a psychedelic idea? No, not at all, not for me. I strongly believe everything I wrote will be possible and can happen. It will happen. To create that world in the future, we start from now, from today – by getting to know people who are transgender, non-binary or LGB. In the distant past, someone imagined the world today and the world is connected closely through technology more than ever in the history of mankind, why won't it be possible that we can also be connected through our consciousness and true knowledge? We certainly will.

The future belongs to us trans people. The future is non-binary.

The article was first published in 'A Man's World' magazine in June 2021.

That's it.

according to

Be the woman

RULE THE

Play the game

your rules.

you wanted to be.

WORLD.

Notes:

Printed in Great Britain
by Amazon